Severe Weather

Hurricanes

by Trudy Becker

FOCUS READERS

SCOUT

www.focusreaders.com

Focus Readers is distributed by North Star Editions:
sales@northstareditions.com | 888-417-0195

Produced for Focus Readers by Red Line Editorial.

Photographs ©: Shutterstock Images, cover, 1, 4, 7, 15 (top), 16 (bottom left), 16 (bottom right); iStockphoto, 8, 11, 12 (top), 12 (bottom), 15 (bottom), 16 (top left), 16 (top right)

Library of Congress Cataloging-in-Publication Data
Names: Becker, Trudy author
Title: Hurricanes / Trudy Becker.
Description: Mendota Heights, MN: Focus Readers, 2026. | Series: Severe weather | Includes index. | Audience: Grades K-1
Identifiers: LCCN 2025022908 (print) | LCCN 2025022909 (ebook) | ISBN 9798889986287 hardcover | ISBN 9798889986355 paperback | ISBN 9798889986485 pdf | ISBN 9798889986423 ebook
Subjects: LCSH: Hurricanes--Juvenile literature
Classification: LCC QC944.2 .B43 2026 (print) | LCC QC944.2 (ebook) | DDC 551.55/2--dc23/eng/20250523
LC record available at https://lccn.loc.gov/2025022908
LC ebook record available at https://lccn.loc.gov/2025022909

Printed in the United States of America
Mankato, MN
012026

About the Author

Trudy Becker lives in Minneapolis, Minnesota.

Table of Contents

What Are Hurricanes? 5

How Hurricanes Form 9

Keep Safe 13

Glossary 16

Index 16

What Are Hurricanes?

Dark clouds fill the sky.

Rain **pours** down.

A big storm comes.

The wind blows hard.

The storm is not safe.

It is a hurricane.

How Hurricanes Form

Hurricanes start at sea.

The air is warm.

The water is warm, too.

Clouds form above the water.

More clouds join.

They **spin**.

The storm moves.

It reaches land.

floodwater

Keep Safe

Hurricanes are strong.

Waves crash.

Wind breaks houses.

Floodwater covers the land.

Go to a safe spot.

Stay inside.

Get away from **windows**.

Stay until the storm passes.

windows

Glossary

floodwater

spin

pours

windows

Index

H

houses, 13

L

land, 10, 13

R

rain, 5

W

wind, 6, 13